300 Affirmations Plus the Essential Techniques to Accelerate Your Results

By Darren Cottingham

Before we start, here's the legal stuff in plain English...

You may experience different results from those implied or stated in this book, depending on your own personal circumstances. Hopefully, they're much better than you ever dreamed. But on the off-chance they're not, you promise you won't turn up at my doorstep demanding to know why.

The purpose of this book is to educate and entertain; there are no guarantees. If you are suffering from an illness, whether physical or psychological, please consult a medical practitioner. I am not a doctor, I'm just a guy who has (successfully) studied and used affirmations for 18 years and wanted to share what I've discovered with you.

Every effort has been made to ensure this book is free from errors or omissions. However, the parties involved in creating and offering this book to you shall not accept responsibility for injury, loss or damage occasioned to any person acting or refraining from action as a result of material in this book whether or not such injury, loss or damage is in any way due to any negligent act or omission, breach of duty or default on the part of those parties.

There are some links in this book to other resources and books. A few of them are affiliate links. This means that if you click them I might earn a small commission if you purchase as a result of the click. This doesn't cost you any extra (for example, Amazon gives me a small rebate if you purchase something via Amazon after clicking on a link, but you pay the same price regardless). I would be grateful if the link means enough to you that you would be happy for this to happen. If you are not comfortable with this, simply search for the book or resource on the internet and bypass the links.

Introduction

This book will help you improve your life. It will give you tips and techniques to fine-tune your subconscious brain and get it working on your side, helping you achieve whatever you want. This book is about affirmations for the practical person who wants to know why and how.

You'll not only get over 300 affirmations to make you immediately more effective in love, wealth, health, your career, spirituality, hobbies and happiness, but you'll learn how to create your own affirmations that are perfectly tailored to what you want.

I will show you how you can be inadvertently sabotaging your affirmations (and your life!). I'll give you techniques to fight depression and cravings. I'll also give you simple tips to do affirmations every day without it impacting on what you do now – that's right, it won't take any extra time out of your day because you can still be productive multitasking your affirmations.

If you have a child at school or university, this book has the perfect chapter for you to help them achieve great grades. If you are studying yourself, there are some rock-solid techniques that will help you improve your memory, understanding and recall.

I'll tell you how I cured my inability to fall asleep using affirmations and a simple visualisation, how I saved for a house in six months, how I boost my confidence before important meetings, and more.

It's probably true that you don't have a huge number of people that constantly build you up and tell you how amazing you really are.

1

Well, you are amazing, and if no one else is telling you this, you can tell yourself. This is what affirmations do. They feed positive, directed thoughts into your subconscious brain so it has the focus and belief to enable you to achieve what you want.

This isn't airy-fairy stuff. You don't have to be 'spiritual' or 'religious' to do affirmations; you just have to want to change your life now. You'll learn the simple, practical solutions I've used for the last 18 years that will help you take control of your life. The best thing about this book, though, is that you will be able to make a difference to your friends. You'll be able to share affirmations with them and teach them.

My goal is to create massive value for you and if you take some of these techniques and it helps you and your friends, I've achieved what I want. I'm grateful to you for downloading this book and I am looking forward to hearing your success stories.

You're probably itching to get to some affirmations straight away. If you really can't wait and want to jump ahead, I recommend at least reading the section *How do affirmations work?* so that you don't do it wrong. Then just dive right on in.

Good luck! Creative massive value in your life.

What is an affirmation?

At the basic level an affirmation is a simple phrase you repeat to yourself (or have someone repeat to you) which defines a positive, present state about what you want to achieve or be.

It can be said aloud or internalised, and it results in your subconscious mind being programmed with a set of beliefs that make it easier to accomplish what you want.

Probably the most famous affirmation is *Every day, in every way, I'm getting better and better* by Émile Coué. He experienced great results with it, but as an affirmation it's not very specific, and therefore it would only work if the person saying it had some context around what 'getting better and better' actually means. An affirmation **must** have some context and meaning for you – you must understand what you want out of the affirmation.

An affirmation is not a prayer (see why later in this book), it's not necessarily a goal (but could be – I explain the difference later), and it's not mindless optimism.

Creating massive value

We're going to get to the affirmations soon (there are over 300 of them, plus all the variations), but first you need to understand how to do affirmations properly to get the best benefit, and how you can create massive value.

You will attain true wealth if you create massive value, and I'm not just talking about monetary wealth. Create massive value for people you have a friendship or relationship with; create massive value for people in clubs, groups and teams you belong to; create massive value for those who work for you or who you work for and with; and create massive value for your children and relatives.

The more people you can positively affect, the wealthier you will be in terms of mental and physical rewards.

Gratitude

Gratitude is probably the single most important practice you can do outside of affirmations. Tony Robbins talks about an 'attitude of gratitude'; Rhonda Byrne, who wrote a brilliant book called *The Secret (click to view)*, also wrote a whole book about gratitude called *The Magic (click to view)*.

When you are grateful for something, your mind is accepting of receiving more of what you are grateful for.

If you find gratitude difficult or emotionally challenging you might be perceiving gratitude as weakness, i.e. if you have to thank someone for helping you, then the fact they helped you means you didn't do it by yourself. If that thought pattern resonates with you, look at it this

way: people *love* to help people. People help others all the time –
friends, strangers, and people they'll never even meet (for example,
by giving to charity). Denying gratitude won't make you strong, it will
make you lonely.

So, I have a gratitude affirmation that I sometimes do when I'm
walking, and I repeat a list in my head all the things I'm grateful for:

*I'm grateful for my friends, I'm grateful for my parents' support, I'm
grateful for my savings, I'm grateful for my health, etc.* You can make
it up on the fly, or you can write one for yourself.

But now, let's get into the nitty-gritty of affirmations.

How do affirmations work?

There's a law of the universe that, unfortunately, you can't avoid: you tend to get what you think about most. Affirmations are targeted thoughts that are used to help you steer your life in a direction that's appealing to you.

People who think about illness and sickness most will most likely be ill and sick. People who think that people are dishonest will most likely experience dishonesty at the hands of others. People who think that everyone is helpful and caring will tend to experience predominantly helpful and caring people.

Once you have this basic understanding of how your brain works, and particularly how your subconscious works, to get you what you want, you now have no excuse to use victim mentality. You are creating your reality, so if you don't like your reality just go about creating another one using positive affirmations (and other techniques and actions) and don't complain – after all, you created this one!

Sure, there will be things that happen to you that are 'bad' and you might not understand why. But you have the tools now to be able to change your situation for the better.

Can you change other people?

When you do affirmations where you want to affect someone else, for example, *My boss respects me*, you are not changing your boss. The change will be in you or the situation you are in and that will be reflected in your boss. You will either change your personality or workplace manner which will change how your boss perceives you, or create an opportunity where he or she learns a new skill to help recognise your contribution, or manifest a situation where your boss is changed (for example, moved to a different department) and replaced with someone else (perhaps even you!), or open up an opportunity for yourself in a new place where your boss does respect you.

You cannot change someone else without them wanting to change. Affirmations help **you** be in control of the situation and react in the most appropriate way.

When can you do affirmations?

Ideally you will do your affirmations while doing nothing else, but I know that that probably isn't practical for many people; most days it's not practical for me. You only need to do them for 10 minutes a day to start seeing results, and you'd be surprised at the kind of downtime you have that you can utilise.

Here are some ways in which you can get some affirmations in without making any major changes. You can do them while:

• Driving (especially when sitting in traffic – I find that tapping on the steering wheel in time with what I'm saying keeps me more focused and less distracted, and people watching probably think I'm singing along with something rather than just inanely talking to myself)

• During the ads on TV – mute the sound (you probably do this anyway)

• Eating (health-based ones work well here, especially ones about mindfully eating food that nourishes you)

• Walking, jogging or cycling (repetitive motions work very well because you can get into a rhythm speaking the affirmations in time with whatever you are doing)

• Listening to music (sing your affirmations – more about this later)

• Cleaning

• Waiting in line at the supermarket

• Ironing

- Travelling in a lift or on an escalator

- In the shower or brushing your teeth (again, repetitive actions work well to keep a mantra going)

- Filling your car with petrol

- And sitting on the toilet (yes, I said it).

Any time that you start to feel despondent, negative or down is a good time to perk yourself up with a few affirmations, too. Eventually this becomes automatic: a negative thought comes into your brain and the affirmation artillery mobilises and gives you an automatic affirmation to win the battle.

What you might find is that most of your available time during the day is spent with other people present. Those people (unless they're your family and you've told them) are unlikely to understand affirmations. You don't want them to think that you've gone mad and are rambling to yourself because they might try to stage some kind of 'intervention' or, at minimum, will stop inviting your daughter around to their kids' birthday parties.

You also don't want them to think that you've got ideas above your station and are telling yourself you are awesome in a self-aggrandising manner. People that don't do affirmations can be afraid of change, and may have tall-poppy syndrome whereby they want to chop you down to keep you at their level. Therefore, if you want to affirm during these times, do it in your head – it still works.

Tools to help you

Forming a habit is the important thing with affirmations. To get the most benefit, doing them every day is essential. Forming a habit can take between three days and a month or two, so it helps if you have some reminders to prompt you. The stronger the emotional pull for you, the quicker you'll do it. First, I'll share how I do it, then I'll give you some other options.

My setup

1) A copy of Good Habits, which is a free iPhone app
2) A list of affirmations written into a Notes entry on my iPhone

Good Habits tracks how many days I've done my affirmations and my score goes back to zero if I miss a day. As I'm from the gaming generation, having my score drop to zero is mortifying. I only mark it off if I've spent at least 10 minutes doing them. Most days I do affirmations while I stretch in the morning.

I have a few affirmations I do automatically, but I have a more extensive list I can choose from depending on what I feel like, or what I feel I need to achieve.

Alternative options to help you remember to do affirmations

- Set yourself an appointment reminder or alarm each day

- Get up 10 minutes earlier and make it the first thing you do

- Make affirmations the thing you (and perhaps your partner) do when the ads come on TV

- Have a specific song you listen to or sing while walking or in the car (this was effective for me and is explained later)

- Have a list you carry around in your purse

- Put a virtual sticky note on your computer desktop

- Tape a list to your car steering wheel

- Try another iPhone app, or an Android app if you're not a fan of Apple – I don't have any suggestions but any appointment reminder or goal-setting software will do the trick

- Record some affirmations using a recording app on your phone, or a Dictaphone or similar device and play them back, repeating them with yourself

- And you can always keep this book on your Kindle or Kindle Reader software on a different device (bookmark or highlight the affirmations you like best).

Mind 'The Gap'

The Gap is the difference between where you want to be and where you are now. Affirmations are the main psychological method we use to close The Gap. You can use visualisation, too, but you must take action to achieve excellent results.

You can expect to get *some* results from affirmations alone, but accompanied by actions they will become more powerful. The great thing about affirmations is that they condition your mind to be more willing to take action. Here are two examples:

1. Meeting more friends

If you want more friends, simply affirming that you are worthy of, and deserve, new friends will dramatically improve your chances of meeting people that will become friends. However, if you never go out, never call anyone, and never go on the internet (effectively shunning human contact), you would have to question your motivation behind doing that particular affirmation in the first place. You must also be committed to follow through with the right actions to support the affirmation.

2. Losing weight

If you want to lose weight, affirming that you are getting lighter might work. It could affect your physiology in a number of ways without you even knowing, such as reducing your hunger cravings or adjusting your metabolism. But if you also combined this with some exercise then you would supercharge your results.

Don't worry, The Gap will close

Don't worry if you're feeling demoralised at how wide The Gap might be for you right now. This is just temporary. The affirmations will make it easier and give you more motivation to act. Therefore make sure you have a written list of your goals, and a list of at least some of the things you can do to achieve them.

The Gap will remind you constantly that it is there, but it will close gradually.

Fighting depression

I am going to simplify what is a very complex problem and really warrants a whole book. Some forms of depression are fairly immune to affirmations, but some can be helped enormously because it's been found that genetics only plays a fifty percent part in whether you have a baseline of happiness or not. That leaves fifty percent available for you to change, and one of the things you can change is your self-talk. There are other things too - and you can read more in the book *The How of Happiness* by Sonja Lyubormirsky - but we'll focus on the affirmations here. I'm not a doctor and this isn't medical advice, so we'll stick to some common sense options that either I or other people have experienced.

At a base level some kinds of depression are caused by repeatedly not being able to do what you want. This cycle starts feelings of frustration and helplessness and those feelings progress to seemingly permanent despair. It's even worse if your sense of self-worth has been eroded. At the root of this depression is not necessarily anything physiological (although, if you are taking medication, eating a poor diet and are overweight/obese, these factors won't be helping).

Therefore, we want to look for affirmations that start addressing the issues that initially caused the depression, plus build up your self-esteem and work on getting perfect body function. The right set of affirmations can deliver results in a matter of days.

How to evaluate what to do

Let's have a look at some questions you can ask yourself so you can go to the most appropriate affirmations. You'll see that below I am not even going to let you acknowledge that D word because acknowledging it gives it more power. As far as I'm concerned, it's a temporary state and you have started the path to becoming healthy.

Is your temporary state there because:

- there is an underlying physiological/physical problem, for example:

- Did you break your spine and are now confined to a wheelchair?

- Are you clinically obese and can't leave the house?

- Do you have some kind of chronic pain?

- you lost your job?

- a loved one died?

- people keep telling you you're not worthy?

- a loved one left you?

- of medication you take for a completely different problem?

- of a reason you don't know?

For all the scenarios above, you will be able to choose some affirmations that will help you change your situation. Even the scenario where you don't know can be addressed by an affirmation – for example, create one about finding ways to enjoy yourself.

The first step is to appreciate that you actually do have a significant life. You are important. Some people depend on you directly and indirectly: your family, your friends, the people that work in the shops that you buy products from, your hairdresser/barber, the guy that cleans your windows, the people that benefit from the taxes you pay, etc. If you have pets, they depend on you, too. If you don't feel that you have significance, choose an affirmation that reminds you that you do.

Next, pick some affirmations that address your core feelings. If you are feeling lonely, choose affirmations that will make you a better friend as well as affirmations that state that you already have friends that care about you. Feel gratitude for this, even if you know you are in The Gap between where you are and where you want to be.

The questions above can each be related to a type of affirmation:

If you have a disability that has restricted your ability to do some of the things you liked doing in the past then you might need to find a new purpose. Choose affirmations that allow you to discover this new direction in your life, for example: *I know what my life purpose is and I joyfully engage in following it*. Note that this affirmation assumes you already are following it because affirmations are more effective when they describe the end result. You might think that you want to affirm about discovering what your new direction is, but that could leave you in a state of discovering and not achieving the discover itself.

If you are overweight and not happy with your appearance, let's address your relationship with food, for example: *I always make healthy food choices*.

If you are in pain, you need to focus on health, strength, flexibility and other affirmations that will get your body functioning more effectively, for example: *My body is constantly healing itself.*

If you lost your job and want another one, focus on making yourself more attractive to employers, for example: *I am a talented asset to any employer.*

If a loved one has died, there is a grieving process and there could be a number of reasons why you are still feeling sad. Say an affirmation like: *Even though we all miss [Person] he/she is now in a much better place and I am so grateful and happy about this.*

If your self-esteem has been eroded and you need to boost your confidence because people have been telling you that you are not worthwhile, try something simple. I almost always start my affirmations with *I am amazing.* It's just a habit and it gets me in the mood for more affirmations.

If a loved one has left you, you could practice gratitude for what you still have, for example: *I am grateful that my friends and relatives provide me with everything I need.*

If you take medication for a specific problem, affirmations to address that problem, or general health affirmations, can be effective. You can choose an affirmation from the list later in the book.

Finally, if you don't know why you are unhappy, use affirmations to combat negative feelings, for example: *I'm constantly learning and implementing new ways to make myself feel happy.*

Also, it's much more difficult to feel depressed if you are standing up and looking up, so try not sitting or lying down.

Fighting cravings and addictions

Chocolate, alcohol, cigarettes, drugs, coffee, Facebook – they can all be addictive, right? The addiction is in the feeling, therefore affirmations to address cravings must focus on changing your feelings about whatever it is you are craving. You could devote a whole book to dealing with addictions. If they are really troubling you then you should definitely do further reading about it as there is not enough room in this book to go into great depth, and I want to mainly focus on high-level concepts.

The problem with using affirmations to rid yourself of, for example, smoking, is that you really don't want to be reminded of smoking or cigarettes at all once you have quit. Therefore you can use quit-smoking-related affirmations up to the day that you quit to help you reduce your reliance on cigarettes, then use affirmations that support general bodily health. The following affirmations will prepare your body for giving up whatever it is that's troubling you.

Eliminating nicotine from my life is simple

I am a non-smoker and free to return to perfect health

As a non-smoker, my self-esteem and self-image are greatly improved

People admire me for stopping smoking

Being free of nicotine makes me feel incredible – more energy, more stamina, more willpower, more pride

Day-by-day I am beating addiction

I am confidently and calmly eliminating smoking from my life and cleansing myself

I am completely committed to becoming clean

Being a non-smoker gives me a great sense of accomplishment and pride

I am much more attractive now that I am a non-smoker

Every day I need one less cigarette until I will never need cigarettes again

It is easy to quit smoking and be smoke-free

Cigarettes taste and smell bad; they repulse me

There are some NLP (neuro-linguistic programming) techniques which can be effective in reducing cravings (read up on submodalities). You can augment those with affirmations, or try affirmations on their own. The affirmations to pick are the ones that directly address how your body reacts to whatever it is you want to get rid of. Again, like with depression, this is simplifying something that could be the subject of a lengthy book, but if we look at some possible underlying reasons for different addictions, you will hopefully be able to apply the reasoning to your own situation:

• Chocolate: it tastes good and the sugar and caffeine make you feel great, ads for chocolate never contain overweight people, the dairy industry tells you cow's milk is good for you.

- Alcohol: social activities and peer pressure (e.g. friends drink and you want to fit in), the feeling of being drunk is liberating, the media has told you that red wine contains antioxidants, you want to temporarily forget some kind of pain, your body is normalised to alcohol abuse, your family abused alcohol and it seems normal.

- Drugs: you are bored with your life, you are trying to forget something, social activities and peer pressure – your friends or people you admire do it.

- Coffee: you like the taste, you don't get enough sleep and need it to wake up, you drink coffee in social activities (peer pressure).

- Facebook and other social media: fear of missing out (FOMO), boredom with your job or life, voyeurism.

Based on that very brief list above, can you identify or uncover underlying reasons for challenging events in your life? In and of themselves, the items above are just things. It's how they make us feel that creates difficulties. Work on changing how you feel about them and you will make a huge difference to your life.

Getting support from others

This leads on nicely from our sections about depression and addictions: will people support you? Of course, affirmations will help, but you want people on your side as well. Again, you have to look at other people's reasons if they don't seem supportive. For example:

You want to give up drinking, but your peer group loves to get absolutely smashed and doesn't want to lose you as part of their group, and they may also not want to feel that you might start judging them for their behaviour.

Your friends and family might be frightened at the process and outcomes – they are anxious about the change. If you feel that you need their support you will have to either get them on your side or temporarily remove them from the equation if you feel they are sabotaging your efforts.

How to avoid sabotaging your affirmations

I briefly talked about how and why other people might sabotage your efforts. Now it's time to deal with you. Your subconscious mind is very powerful at giving you exactly what it wants. Affirmations consciously influence your subconscious mind, but if you feed it an affirmation that contradicts a strongly held belief, you will find it hard to get any great success with that affirmation. A better technique is to address the core underlying belief with a different affirmation.

For every affirmation you choose, ask yourself 'Is it OK if this affirmation comes true?' You will be surprised how your core beliefs can sometimes contradict what you might consciously desire. Here are a few examples of how you can subconsciously sabotage what you think you want.

Let's say you want to lose weight, therefore you choose an affirmation like *My body burns fat easily and I am becoming slimmer every day*. Let's say you have a partner who is also overweight. If you lose weight and your partner doesn't, would this cause tension? It might be that you subconsciously fear that your partner may become jealous if other people find you attractive; you might think that you would become more attractive to other people, and that could put strain on your relationship because you would be tempted; it might be that your partner finds you attractive being large and has previously said to you that slimmer people are not so attractive (this may or may not be true); it might be that your culture promotes large body sizes as a sign of status and wealth and you don't want to be slim if that means your peers may think of you as being poor or less worthy.

23

Maintaining the love you feel for your partner is important, therefore making this affirmation come true would cause you pain. Your subconscious knows this, but your conscious might not tell you.

There is still benefit in doing this affirmation – you will probably lose some weight – but to supercharge it, make sure you address the underlying problem. In this case you might also choose affirmations related to the quality of your relationship so that you can strengthen your bonds.

Sabotaging your wealth

Looking at your parents' attitude to money will give you a good indication of whether you are sabotaging your own wealth. If you were told any of the following statements when you were a child, you will need to address them first:

- Money doesn't grow on trees

- You have to work hard to earn money

- I'm not made of money

- It's virtuous to be poor

- Money is the root of all evil.

Let's deal with these negative thoughts. Firstly, money does grow on trees if you own an orchard; and if you don't own an orchard, you can at least put your money in a bank *branch* (OK, less of the puns). Second, there are millions of people who don't work that hard for their money; they work smart. Third, no one is made of money, but everyone makes their money. Fourth, many religions (wrongly) teach us it's not good to be rich (I deal with this in the organised religion section later), but you can do a lot more good with money than without it, all other things being equal. Finally, it's the love of money that's a root of some evil, not money itself.

There is more on this topic in the section titled *Check they align with your deeper beliefs and values.*

Cultural and gender sabotage

Some cultures, for example, certain Pacific Island and Asian cultures, are very humble. An affirmation is anything but humble! An affirmation is a bold statement of accomplishment that differentiates you from where you are now.

There can be hidden fears that if you suddenly start accomplishing these major goals and making your life much better that you will no longer belong to your peer group.

Other cultures are not supportive of women's rights, and want women to believe they can't accomplish (or shouldn't accomplish) as much as men.

Do you have any cultural ties that could slow down the progress you make with affirmations?

Affirmation frustration

Your mind can become jaded with certain affirmations and they can lose their effectiveness. Changing the wording of affirmations after a few months can help you achieve better results.

You can move on to completely different affirmations that mean something similar or you can play with the wording of your affirmations. Be sure to check out the *Constructing your own affirmations* section.

Keeping it real

We should all aim high in our affirmations, but we should do so realistically. None of the eight finalists in the Olympic 100m sprint would have told themselves they couldn't win and that it was impossible to win. All will be using affirmations (along with other techniques), and taking massive action. However, only one will win.

However much I affirm it, I will never be the first female ruler of Saudi Arabia (I'm not female, for one), or be 25 again. I probably wouldn't even be able to reverse male pattern baldness (although, I should give it a go). Your affirmations must be ultimately physically or mentally possible within the constraints of this world.

You *can* improve your health, wealth, memory, fitness, relationships, friendships, living circumstances, sporting abilities, compassion, empathy, vocabulary, and ability to hold your breath underwater. In fact, you can do pretty much anything. You just need to consider the rules and restrictions of the system in which we live.

Are affirmations goals?

Affirmations are often expressed in a way that sounds like you've already achieved a goal, but they aren't the goal itself. A goal should be SMART (Specific, Measurable, Achievable/Attainable, Relevant [some people say Realistic] and Time-constrained). Affirmations will help you achieve your goals.

For example, if your goal is to buy a new car there will be a certain set of actions that need to be taken and you can affirm for each action, or you can affirm for the final goal (or both).

Action to take	Sample affirmation
Deciding which car to buy	*I am choosing a car that is perfect for my requirements*
Saving for the car	*Every week I am earning enough to save for my car*
Buying the car	*My new car is mechanically perfect, everything is right and it is a bargain.*

The final affirmation is by far the most powerful. It tells your subconscious brain that you already have the new car and your subconscious will, in turn, help your conscious brain make it a reality.

Are prayers affirmations?

Prayers tend to ask a different entity for help and put your destiny in its hands. Affirmations directly state to yourself what you are achieving and make you responsible for it.

The basic tenet of this book is that you are in control. However, I believe there is some kind of higher power, other entity, gestalt consciousness or something that I don't understand and can't prove, that binds all things together in this universe, whether you call it God, Allah or something else. I can't describe it to you because I don't know what it is for sure; I don't want to convince you to believe the same as me because my opinions are the sum total of my learning so far, and I might be wrong or my opinion might change when I get new information.

This book does not say that there is no higher power doing something within your life and having some kind of role, but if you put **all** your faith in a higher power or other entity to deliver everything you need, do you even need affirmations? Or do affirmations simply bring you closer to whatever it is you believe? Perhaps whatever it is out there plays an active part in hearing what you are saying and holds you accountable for your actions in achieving your goals and dreams.

The point of this chapter is to say that a prayer is not an affirmation, but that doesn't mean an affirmation wouldn't necessarily be heard or influenced by a higher power (if that is part of your belief structure).

Techniques

Music

I decided to save for my first house in June 1996. I wanted to have that house by Christmas 1996, so I started looking at how I could cram affirmations into my 70-hour work week. The only feasible time was the half-hour I spent every day driving to and from work.

I picked a tune that had recently been popular that had a simple hook for the chorus – *Peaches* by The Presidents of the United States of America. I can hear some of you groaning already. The actual chorus says:

"Movin' to the country,

Gonna eat a lot of peaches

Movin' to the country,

Gonna eat me a lot of peaches

Movin' to the country,

Gonna eat a lot of peaches

Movin' to the country,

Gonna eat a lot of peaches"

Those are pretty average lyrics as far as creativity goes because that's the whole chorus. However, it did give me the opportunity to sing exactly the same melody to myself with:

30

"Savin' lots of money

Gonna buy myself a townhouse"

Rinse and repeat.

This became an earworm for me for several months until on the last working day before Christmas 1996 at 4:30pm I signed the documents to my new house. It was unbelievable the things that fell into place to allow this to happen.

In a way, my naivety at affirmations had worked far too well. I got a house, but I didn't put any other parameters around it and it didn't work out to be the best house. However, it proved to me that affirmations are extremely powerful and music is a way of accelerating their effectiveness.

If you want to sing your affirmations you can develop your own melodies, 'borrow' your favourite melodies, accompany yourself on guitar, rap the lyrics – use your own creativity.

You can do affirmations in the shower, while you're doing things around the house, while you're in the car, and so on. Initially, you might feel a little embarrassed, but this wears off and eventually it'll be very natural.

If you want to do affirmations with your family, choose something you all want, like a holiday to a theme park or a new house. Bear in mind that teenagers may ridicule you for this, so pick your battles.

Meditation

There are a few different types of meditation and I have to admit that I'm useless at pretty much all of them. If I sit down quietly then I'll more than likely fall asleep. However, don't let that put you off because if you either like the idea of meditating or can meditate then you can use an affirmation as a mantra.

Personally I only feel comfortable using affirmations when doing a walking meditation and I say the affirmation each step (or in time with my steps). I don't do this very often because I prefer walking for fitness (which is a different kind of walking), and I often do affirmations then anyway, if I'm not listening to podcasts.

Visualisation

It's not essential to visualise anything when you are doing affirmations, but if you do, it can help. If you want that new car, imagine yourself driving it while doing your affirmations; if you want to have a positive relationship with your daughter, visualise it while you are doing the affirmation.

There's a whole different school of thought that says visualisation works as well as affirmation. Therefore, visualisation plus affirmation might work twice as well!

Mirror work

Louise Hay teaches a technique where you look at a mirror while doing your affirmations. Look into your own eyes and say the affirmations. For some people this can be an emotional and difficult experience at the start.

Why would this work? As well as thinking about the words and hearing yourself say the affirmation you are seeing yourself say it too. Think about what was just said about visualisation and how powerful that is. You are seeing an image of yourself reinforcing what you want to be.

Writing

Writing is consistently rated as one of the best ways to remember something. All you need is a bit of paper and a couple of affirmations you'd like to work on. First thing in the morning, or last thing at night, write each affirmation a few times. If I use this technique, I prefer the morning because I'm less likely to fall asleep while doing them.

While you're writing it, you'll be thinking about it, and because writing is slower, you spend slightly more time on each thought. Typing doesn't seem to work as well as writing in the old analogue way.

If you put them in a diary or journal, then you can build a book of positive thoughts that you will have started and/or ended your day with.

I pretty much only use this technique for business affirmations because I always have a pen and paper handy. It's usually when something has not gone as I expected. Rather than be annoyed about it, I bring out the big guns to beat back the negative thought and write what I'm going to make happen instead. That switches my mood back to being optimistic and it's business as usual.

Teaching and partnering

I find the single best way to learn something inside out is to have to teach it to someone else. If you've got kids, they're a good place to start, especially if you have a shared goal. If you manage to get yours to love washing the dishes, please let me know.

Initially you might feel a little shy saying them in front of other people, especially because, due to The Gap, you'll be saying something that isn't 'reality' (whatever that is) in that particular moment.

Something that can make this easier is to have your partner or friend say the affirmation directed at you and you repeat it. For example:

Your partner/friend: *You are empathetic and caring*

You: *I am empathetic and caring*

Repeat this several times (10-15) and then some other affirmations, too. There's a strong likelihood some affirmations done this way will make you feel quite vulnerable. Those affirmations are often the ones you most need.

Now you should reverse the process doing it for your friend. Notice how it feels much different. Saying those affirmations to someone else is empowering. It makes you feel great!

There is an opportunity here to practice gratitude and affirmations:

Your partner/friend: *I'm really grateful that you are an amazing friend*

You: *I am an amazing friend*

Remember to switch after you've done a few. This technique can really build a friendship or relationship, as long as you both have mutual trust.

The affirmations

All affirmations in this section are in *italics*. There are a lot of them – around 300 base affirmations, and you can add the ones peppered through the book. Plus, I'm giving you the tools to create your own ones, so technically there are thousands just in the variations in these pages.

To give you the best value for your money, I have tried not to duplicate affirmations across the sections. Even if you are only looking for health-based affirmations, check out the other sections, too, because there might be wording in them which you can apply to your own requirements using the **critical success factors** for each section.

Each section of affirmations is presented alphabetically.

Relationships

Our interactions with other people can sometimes become strained and communication can be difficult. Affirmations can give you clarity in your mind about these relationships. It might be time to let go, time to heal wounds, or time to build stronger friendships.

This section covers affirmations that are aimed at those of you already in relationships, and those looking for a relationship.

Relationship affirmations

All my relationships are long-lasting and loving

Being compassionate and considerate is one of my top priorities

Everyone acts with good intent

I accept a perfect, loving relationship

I accept apologies with compassion and forgiveness

I act like the person I want to become

I always speak kindly of other people

I am a consistent, reliable friend that is always there when people need me

I am an honest and devoted partner

I am attractive and engaging

I am creating rewarding relationships every day

I am creating room in my life for my soul mate

I am enjoying a fabulous relationship with a person that adores and loves me

I am generous and giving of my time and resources

I am grateful for the relationships I already have in my life and the ones I will have

I am immensely happy to be in a relationship with my soul mate

I am more in love every day

I am ready to accept the perfect partner into my life

I am sexier now than I have ever been

I am supremely confident meeting new men/women

I am worthy of love

I attract positive people into my life

I deserve the perfect partner and a beautiful relationship

I easily remember names and faces

I empower people and make them feel great about themselves

I enjoy making love and being intimate

I feel attractive and proud of myself

I have a caring wife/husband/boyfriend/girlfriend

I have an excellent relationship with my wife/husband/kids/boyfriend/girlfriend

I have awesome friends that care about me

I make friends easily because I can quickly find common ground

I see the world and the people in it through eyes of love and acceptance

It's easy to meet interesting men/women who find me attractive

It's OK to have my own beliefs and I accept that others are entitled to have their beliefs

My boyfriend/girlfriend/wife/husband/lover is the most attractive person in the world

My friends love spending time with me

My life is filled with passion and romance

My words and actions build stronger bonds with people I care about

My work and home life are in perfect harmony

People are interested in me because I am interesting

The more I love myself, the more attractive I become to other people

When people share their feelings, I am a compassionate and understanding listener

Women/men find me very attractive

Critical success factors

To make up your own affirmations here are some words that can be substituted into the affirmations above. It's not intended to be an exhaustive list – feel free to add your own words.

Love, acceptance, husband, wife, children, relatives, friends, bonds, relationships, beliefs, harmony, beauty, attractiveness, feelings, soul mate, partner, mate, sex, sexy, men, women, attracting.

Wealth and abundance

As you'll read in the section about aligning your affirmations with your deeper beliefs and values, wealth can polarise people. On the surface they want wealth, but deep down they might be harbouring beliefs that wealth is not good.

Wealth won't necessarily make you any happier long term (in fact, it's proven to have very little impact at all on your actual happiness over time), but it does allow you to make choices to increase the happiness and wellbeing of other people.

Wealth and abundance affirmations

A constant and increasing stream of abundance flows towards me

Abundance comes to me easily

Every day I am grateful for the abundance in my life and all around me

Every day I attract more abundance and wealth by improving my skills and talents

Every day I create more and more wealth

Every day I take positive action to achieve more wealth

Every positive thought and affirmation brings greater abundance to me both physically and spiritually

Everything I want and need is within my abilities to obtain

I allow abundance to flow freely throughout every positive aspect of my life

I always get what I deserve, and my actions and positive thoughts are always improving what I deserve

I am creating massive value

I am entitled to joy, happiness and abundance

I am entitled to receive great wealth - both physical and spiritual - in my life

I am inspired by people who have abundance, and I inspire other people to greater abundance

I am open to receiving the fruits of my efforts and affirmations

I am positively influencing others and that, in return, brings more wealth to me

I am ready to receive more money

I am surrounded by a world that has infinite opportunities for me to grasp

I am surrounded by riches and opportunity

I am worthy of abundance in my whole life

I create happiness and abundance for myself and those I care about

I deserve abundance

I deserve to be rich and I accept money into my life

I enjoy happiness, wealth and abundance

I find opportunities everywhere

I give thanks for the riches in my life

I have everything I need to create massive wealth

I live in a rich and abundant universe

I naturally think in terms of increasing my abundance

I recognise that by increasing the abundance of others, I will naturally increase my own abundance

I relax and allow the universe to assist me to obtain the things I want and need

I strongly attract wealth into my life

I welcome physical and spiritual riches into my life

Infinite abundance follows me everywhere

It's OK to be rich

Money is good; I do good things with money

My mind is focused on and successful at achieving success and wealth

Staggering wealth is ready for me to grasp

The universe will provide riches and wealth as I continue to develop and improve

The wealthier I am, the more I can help other people

There is immense abundance and riches available to me

Today I claim the wealth and riches that I deserve

Today I see and feel the wealth and riches I am entitled to

Critical success factors

Wealth, abundance, unlimited, deserving, opportunities, influencing, physical wealth, spiritual wealth, richness, actions, fortune, luck, gratitude, confidence.

Career, business growth and success

Whether you are an employee or an employer you will experience challenges and setbacks. Some setbacks can be particularly challenging and demoralising, like an unexpected redundancy.

Imagine you've sunk all your money and more into a project and you have the promise of venture capital investment from a huge multinational company and then some idiot orders a couple of aeroplanes to be flown into the World Trade Center, the promised money disappears and you lose all yours overnight.

Not to trivialise the events of 9/11, but that did happen to me and it took a while to build it back up again. In the quest for business or career success, some days are going to suck. At least I didn't lose a loved one; at least I still had optimism and affirmations on my side.

There are two affirmations I regularly use before meetings: *I always know the right thing to say* and one of John Kehoe's ones, *I am powerful, persuasive, creative and productive.* I have found I achieve generally better results if I repeat these a few times before going into a meeting. I also use techniques as described in Amy Cuddy's TED talk about body language, which you can find on YouTube.

The following affirmations are relevant for employees, team members, team leaders and company owners. Use the critical success factors section at the end to build your own affirmations, too.

Career, business growth and success affirmations

Action leads to positive results, and I love results

45

Every action I take moves me closer to my goals

Great money-making ideas come to me every day

I always achieve my goals

I always know which actions will return the greatest rewards and benefits

I am a brilliant businessman/businesswoman/entrepreneur

I am a spring of brilliant, profitable ideas

I am a nurturing and supportive manager and colleague

I am an excellent speaker and can competently stand up for what I believe

I am completely at ease taking on new challenges and roles

I am confident and capable in all my business dealings

I am confident and self-assured in all situations

I am dedicated and persistent

I am deserving of a promotion and a raise

I am excellent at planning

I am good enough for a promotion

I am grateful for my career and abilities

I am immensely grateful for the wonderful customers that support my business

I am powerful and persuasive

I am respected by my peers and colleagues

I am winning the respect and business of new clients every week

I believe in myself and my company/employer

I can see my dreams and I naturally convert this to the right actions

I deal with people using integrity and honesty and they recognise this

I demonstrate my commitment to my staff/boss/team

I do the important things first

I have infinite energy to build my company, and the belief to make it successful

I have lots of sales and success every day

I have strong visual ideas of success

I know exactly what to say in a job interview to impress the interviewer

I plan my day and it follows the plan

I think clearly before I react, even in high-pressure situations

I thrive under pressure

I trust myself to do an amazing job and over-deliver on my clients' expectations

I trust that all situations arise for a reason, and that reason is always the perfect reason

I vibrate success and attract rewarding and profitable clients

I'm inspired to take action every day

My boss respects me

My business is growing rapidly

My communication skills are superb and I convey my meaning with quiet self-assurance

My company is competitive and respected

My positivity rubs off on my colleagues, managers and direct reports and helps us achieve greater business success

Critical success factors

Actions, positivity, strategy, planning, competitiveness, acumen, business nous, clients, sales, success, teamwork, respect, promotion, tenacity, persuasiveness, drive, ideas, confidence, communication, customers, products, services.

Personal growth and spirituality

If you're at all like me you'll start to see that there's so much you want to improve about yourself, so where do you start? The best approach to personal growth is to pick one area and focus on it rather than a less effective shotgun approach. If you're already pretty happy with yourself, hone in on fine-tuning your awesomeness.

Personal growth and spirituality affirmations

Every day I become more in tune with my body and aware of my emotions

Every day I experience the positive feelings that affirmation and visualisation bring

Giving freely to others makes me feel amazing and I know it will be returned to me many times

Helping others gives my life more meaning

I accept 100% responsibility for everything in my life

I accept all comments and feedback as positive information that helps me grow

I accept and love myself completely

I accept life as a rewarding, empowering experience

I accept my emotions and choose to only nurture the positive ones

I allow myself to feel all the positive things my life offers me

I always allow my true feelings to guide me

I always remember names and faces

I am an empathetic and caring person who completely understands what other people need

I am calm and relaxed in all situations

I am completely at peace with the past, knowing that I can only change the future

I am creative and full of incredible ideas

I am grateful for everything in my life

I am grateful for the knowledge and willingness to improve every aspect of myself

I am in command of my emotional responses

I am the only person who controls my feelings

I can switch my emotional state in an instant to be productive, positive and empowered

I choose honest, positive emotions

I commit to developing powerful and beneficial personal character traits

I control my reactions to situations in my life

I effortlessly replace negative emotions with positive ones and change my emotional state quickly

I feel fantastic and know that my thoughts align with my goals and wishes

I find humour and knowledge in the adversity that makes me more resilient and more capable in life

I focus my energy on peaceful and positive emotions and reactions

I gain new wisdom from each challenge and apply it to solve future challenges quickly

I give 100% commitment to my goals

I give myself permission to grow spiritually

I have complete control over my inner dialogues, feelings, images and thoughts

I improve my spiritual and emotional being by becoming more aware of my personal beliefs

I love and respect my feelings and my connection to spirit

I love being in control of how I feel

It is safe to see others' point of view

It's OK to be me

My emotions are always appropriate for any given situation

My emotions teach me what I need to grow

My feelings all provide valuable insights about my deeper beliefs

My life brings me happiness and joy

My mood is always uplifting and inspires others to be happy

My positive mood is resistant and resilient against the moods of others

My positive thoughts improve my positive returns from life

My spiritual path is full of valuable learnings and amazing people

My subconscious mind is my partner in success

Critical success factors

Thoughts, feelings, reactions, experiences, emotions, situations, positivity, calmness, beliefs, self-control, empowering, any word you use to describe your God or divine being, responsibility, acceptance, possibilities, good, peace, desires, warmth, kindness, compassion, generosity, fortune, humanity, thoughtfulness, charity, giving, gratitude, faith.

Memory and academic success

I wasn't particularly successful at school. Despite having amazingly supportive parents, I was painfully shy and barely able to say my name in roll call. I was occasionally bullied and sometimes quite scared. I was above average, but definitely not top of the class. I barely scraped into university and went for a day, ending up at a technical college where I met an amazing friend who gave me my first book on affirmations. I don't remember the name of the book, but it gave me enough information to start making up my own. Here's the main affirmation I created for studying. It's a simple four-word affirmation that saw me get 90% or more for every written exam with minimal study.

Perfect memory, perfect recall

It seems to have resulted in me having a better-than-normal memory which is great for me...and occasionally annoying for others.

There are three main areas that affect studying: attitude, memory and understanding.

Attitude towards studying

If you don't want to study, there are potentially several reasons:

- You don't want the things that study will give you badly enough

- You had a bad experience at school, e.g. bullying

- You have come to associate education with being ostracised or uncool, etc.

If you identify with any of these, choose affirmations that address them – ones related to setting goals, making friends more easily, or the fact that after school, being smart makes it easier to be popular because you have more choices and awareness.

Memory

You have to remember facts. While this might seem terribly 19th century in this day and age of perpetual connection to the internet, retaining facts allows you to make informed decisions and more. Knowledge is power (and doesn't require Wi-Fi).

There are basic factors here, too. If you always study with music on, when you get into an exam scenario where you can't have music playing, your brain will find it harder to recall the information. If you have a diet high in sugar (and even worse, snack on sugary foods during an exam), it's the equivalent of putting sand in your car's petrol tank. Don't disadvantage your memory.

Understanding

When you successfully apply the facts you have memorised to a situation or problem, you've achieved understanding.

Insert the name of the subject you are studying into the memory affirmations wherever you see [subject].

Memory affirmations

Any information I need to recall comes effortlessly to me

I always feel inspired to write great assignments

I always find the knowledge I need when I need it

I always hand my assignments and homework in on time

I always present logical arguments and concrete analysis in my coursework

I always remember what I hear and read

I am calm, relaxed and 100% focused in exams

I am confident I know my subject

I am developing a strong mind

I am grateful for my excellent memory

I am top of the class in [subject]

I am very productive every time I study

I can concentrate for as long as I want to

I concentrate easily

I deeply understand questions and tasks immediately and respond with perfect answers and solutions

I enjoy finishing tasks and achieving goals

I enjoy getting smarter

I feel creative, motivated and focused at school

I feel empowered when I learn something new

I have a clear mind with razor-sharp thinking

I have a photographic memory with unlimited storage

I have an amazing memory that remembers and recalls everything I see, hear and experience

I have an incredible memory

I have awesome goals that I know will come true when I'm successful at studying

I have perfect access to my past experiences and knowledge

I have willpower and dedication

I love learning new facts

I remain focused for long periods of time

I remember to write important facts down

I trust my memory to provide all the information I require

I use all my senses to help me memorise and recall information easily

Learning [subject] is easy and fun

My brain develops positive connections and understands new knowledge rapidly

My brain loves new information

My memory for facts and figures is excellent

My memory improves every day

My mind perfectly stores everything I read

My mind processes information quickly

My reports and assignments are clearly written and logically presented. I find writing them is easy

My teachers are supportive

Perfect memory, perfect recall

The more I use my memory the better it gets

Critical success factors

Attitude, memory, understanding, recall, fact-finding, mastery, writing, information, facts, subjects, assignments, tasks, details, knowledge, experiences, clarity.

Health and wellbeing

If you're looking for addiction-related affirmations, they're in an earlier section that deals with cravings and addictions. The following affirmations are targeted toward general health, strength and healthy habits.

It's important to note that what the media and food companies say is healthy is often not actually healthy - just less unhealthy than alternatives. Make yourself a student of the truth about food because it is the fuel for your body.

You could fill a whole book on how specific affirmations can help different ailments. Here's one I had success with.

I used to have extremely poor sleep quality. I used the affirmation *I fall asleep quickly* along with a visualisation that I was walking down stairs leading to a dark basement to train my body from taking sometimes more than an hour to go to sleep to taking less than 30 seconds. This took less than a fortnight.

I am currently experimenting with affirmations to help myself stay asleep because I tend to wake up a few times in the night. There might be a physiological cause (some kind of sleep apnoea), but I haven't had this diagnosed yet. The longest I've stayed asleep in one stretch is seven hours, whereas it's typical for me to wake momentarily after four hours, then two or three times more between two and four hours later. I rarely lie awake – it's a brief moment where I know I've woken, then I fall back to sleep.

I have read that it is natural for your body to have a period of wakefulness after four to five hours, therefore I'm not overly worried about waking up several times in the night. However, if you are suffering insomnia (i.e. you can't get to sleep in the first place), try the technique I mentioned above, plus consider what the underlying cause might be (old bed, noisy environment, snoring partner, ingesting stimulants too late in the day, etc).

Health and wellbeing affirmations

All excess fat is melting away from my body

Being beautiful is as simple as thinking beautiful thoughts towards people

Daily exercise invigorates me and makes me feel great

Eternal youth surges through my body

Every day I develop new, positive, healthy habits

Every day my body is replenished

I acknowledge and accept my body's perfection

I always do what's best for my body

I am a beautiful, happy person

I am changing my habits by changing my thought patterns

I am cured and healed

I am proud of my healthy lifestyle

I am ready to do what it takes to be healthy

I choose to feel fantastic about myself and how I look

I easily overcome unhealthy habits and replace them with healthy habits

I enjoy being fit and trim

I fall asleep quickly and easily

I feel so grateful for every day I make healthy choices

I feel young and full of youthful energy and vitality

I have thick, luxurious, healthy hair

I have beautiful fresh breath

I honour my body in every way possible

I love breathing clean, fresh air and feeling calm and relaxed

I love my body and my body naturally knows what to do to be healthy

I only use food to satisfy legitimate hunger

I radiate youthfulness and health

My body achieves perfect balance and harmony

My body has incredible healing powers

My body is full of radiant health and youthful energy

My body is growing younger and healthier

My body only wants healthy foods and only in the quantities it needs

My body regenerates itself based on a perfect template

My body rejects drugs - I am clean and healthy**

My digestive system efficiently absorbs all the nutrients I need

My eyesight is perfect and my eyes are strong

My healthy eating habits support my body's desire to remain youthful

My hearing is acute and finely attuned to quiet sounds

My joints and muscles are relaxed, flexible and feel great

My life is dynamic, rewarding and fun

My skin is supple, clear and radiant

The cells in my body are returning to their original blueprint

Today is one step closer to complete and total health

Today, I only put healthy things in my body

**Only use this one up to the point of giving up drugs.

Critical success factors

Action, exercise, goals, results, health, wellbeing, youthfulness, vibrancy, habits, willpower, strength, balance, harmony, beauty, attractiveness.

Sports success

With the following affirmations you can swap out the word 'sport' and insert the name of the sport you want to be good at, whether it's golf, badminton or that one where you run down a hill alongside big wheels of cheese (something that will probably never be in the Olympics).

I have included some critical success factors for different sports after the affirmations for you to construct your own affirmations.

Sports affirmations

Every day I become faster, stronger and more focused

Exercise makes my body feel powerful

Exercise tones my body and improves my self-esteem

Exercising daily improves my mood

I accept responsibility for, and am proud of, my place in the team

I always have more luck than my competitors

I always know what's best for the team

I always perform my best and give 100%

I always reach my training goals

I am a fierce competitor

I am a fountain of energy

I am a great athlete

I am a natural-born sportsman/sportswoman

I am a winner

I am accurate and focused with astoundingly quick reactions

I am agile and flexible

I am attaining all my sporting goals

I am committed to playing sport

I am more determined, more capable and more cunning than my competition

I am motivated to practice

I deserve success in my sport

I enjoy playing sport

I feel youthful and full of energy when playing sport

I have everything I need to succeed in my sport

I have excellent coordination

I have the mental edge to dominate my competition

I have the skill to beat my opponents

I inspire my team and my team responds with greatness

I intimidate my competition

I stay focused on winning

I take advantage of every opportunity my competitors miss

I throw/pitch/kick/drive with speed, accuracy and power

I visualise the win and it happens naturally

My body is built for sports and winning

My endurance is naturally high

My natural sporting talents improve every time I play

My stamina is increasing

My teammates respect my skills and abilities

Playing sport comes naturally to me

Playing sports balances my emotions and makes me happier

Practicing my sport gives me the confidence to win

Winning feels great - I love winning and I can win

Critical success factors

Golf
Accurate swing, drive length, putting accuracy, choice of club, keeping it on the green/fairway, perfect stance, finding the perfect caddy.

Motorsports
Fast reactions, strategic driving, taking the chequered flag, making the gap, posting consistent lap times, qualifying on pole position, making a great start (holeshot into the first corner), overtaking skill, supportive team, reliable vehicle, excellent strategy.

Take care when affirming about having a damage-free race or avoiding collisions as technically these are drawing your attention to damage and collisions. Be sure to visualise exactly what you mean when you affirm so that there's no ambiguity.

Ball sports (soccer, rugby, American football, basketball, etc.)
Passing accuracy, shooting speed, teamwork, defending/blocking, stamina, running speed, team success, supportive manager, coordination, self-belief.

Bat and ball sports (cricket, baseball, tennis, etc.)
Hitting accuracy, throwing speed and accuracy, teamwork, catching ability, running speed, team success, supportive manager, coordination, self-belief.

Endurance sports (running, cycling, swimming)
Strength, flexibility, stamina, speed, mental strength.

Constructing your own affirmations

There is a set of very simple rules for creating your own effective affirmations:

1. Never use negatives

2. Never use 'I want'

3. Keep them simple

4. Make them emotionally charged

5. Make them in the present

6. Check they align with your deeper beliefs and needs (do you really want it in all circumstances?)

Never use negatives...I mean, always use positives

You'll notice that none of the affirmations in this book says don't, not, no or nothing. Your subconscious mind doesn't understand negatives; it takes everything you throw at it positively. If you affirm 'I am not fat', what your subconscious mind hears is 'I am fat'. If you affirm 'I am not poor', what your subconscious mind hears is 'I am poor'.

It's often easiest for you to identify what is wrong with your life by using a negative – you might be in pain, have a bad relationship with your children, be living in a dangerous neighbourhood, or be unable to donate to charity.

The first thing that might come to your mind could be a statement like 'I don't want my back to hurt'. To make an affirmation you must turn the statement around to positively state the outcome you want. But here's a trap for beginners - you might think that the opposite of pain is pain-free. Technically it is, but not to your subconscious mind, which will associate 'pain-free' as being connected with pain. You can choose from a number of more positive statements and build a statement that feels right for you. For example:

My back functions perfectly

Every day, my back feels fantastic

My back is relaxed and strong

My back is perfect

Never use 'I want'

If you use 'I want', that will keep you in a perpetual state of wanting and not having. Using 'I want' keeps you in The Gap, never achieving the end goal. It's the same as using 'I wish'.

Short and simple

The value of affirmations is in their repetition and easy ability to be understood and assimilated by your subconscious. If you are new to affirmations you should choose short and simple phrases that you can easily remember and recall while you are out. Once you get more adept at affirmations you can make compound phrases that have more depth.

I had a fairly long affirmation and I think I got it from a seminar that was by Kurek Ashley, who is a great motivational speaker, former movie star, and record-holding fire walker. It was a whole paragraph, and just a little too long for me. I like to regularly change my affirmations and this paragraph was too onerous to recreate in different forms. In my opinion, the value in affirmations is the simple repetition which hammers the message home.

Make them emotionally charged

If your affirmations have a strong emotion attached to them, they tend to be more effective and more easily achievable. Just make sure it's not a negative emotion, e.g. if you're affirming for health you don't want to dwell on the negative aspects of why you're doing that affirmation; focus on how awesome and liberating it will feel when you are better.

Keep them in the present

The 'I am...' statement is the most powerful statement and one of the easiest to construct (for example, *I am tremendously successful*). You can also use:

'I have...' (for example, *I have a caring wife*)

'I find...' (for example, *I find opportunities everywhere*)

'My...' (for example, *My boss respects me*)

'I always...' (for example, *I always have more luck than my competitors*)

'I feel...' (for example, *I feel so grateful for every day I make healthy choices about smoking*)

'I know…' (for example, *I know exactly what to say in a job interview to impress the interviewer*)

'I love…' (for example, *I love practicing piano*)

'I allow…' (for example, *I allow abundance and wealth into my life*)

'I accept…' (for example, *I accept who I am now and enjoy becoming a better person*)

'I welcome…' (for example, *I welcome and acknowledge positive feelings and energy every day*)

'I choose…' (for example, *I choose to feel good about myself and how I look*)

Check they align with your deeper beliefs and values

I already covered some of this in the *How to avoid sabotaging your affirmations* section. This is easiest to illustrate with an example, although it's difficult in practice to figure out what your core beliefs are without asking yourself very searching questions.

You will find it very difficult to be rich if your core belief is that money is evil. You can affirm all you like, but a conflict with your subconscious will deliver substandard results. How will you know this? You can ask yourself a few questions to get to the bottom of it. Here are a few, but you might think of more:

1. What's your gut reaction to the concept of (in this case) making a huge amount of money – does it worry you that you might have more responsibilities, more risk, etc?

2. What is your language around the concept, e.g. do you use 'filthy lucre' and does that mean your concept of money is dirty?

3. What have your parents told you, e.g. money doesn't grow on trees, and you have to work hard?

4. What are your peers' attitudes to money, e.g. do they have a poverty or scarcity mentality, and do they look down on people with money?

5. What have your religious/spiritual teachers told you, e.g. money is the root of all evil, and you can't buy happiness?

Those are just five questions. It's surprising anyone's rich at all, right! To be rich, you have to be comfortable with being rich, believe that it's OK for you to be rich, and see being rich as being better than being poor (because you can help more people).

Now apply those kinds of questions to all the challenges in your life.

Taking it to the next level: fine-tuning the inputs to your brain

You might be thinking by now that I sound like I do affirmations all the time. The answer couldn't be further from the truth. My brain is also full of random thoughts, catchy tunes that I can't get rid of, ponderings about what to eat for lunch and whether to buy a new pair of socks because one sock has a hole in it, or should I find a needle and thread and fix it.

I (mostly) do ten minutes of affirmations in the morning and the rest of the time they just come as an automatic response to some kind of negative stimulus –a regular, positive diet of self-talk rather than a structured session of affirmations. They're like the martial artist who can deflect the blow rather than be knocked down by it. They are also my automatic response when I hear things that are blatant rubbish or designed to make me feel bad about myself.

The more you do affirmations the more you'll want to do them because you'll start seeing results and then you'll start seeing more things you want to fix! I see a huge number of areas I'd like to (and some would say *need to*) work on, particularly around personal relationships. For you, it might be different.

By now you're probably starting to realise that if *you* can manually input good stuff into your brain then it means that *other people* can deliberately or inadvertently input bad stuff into your brain.

When I realised this myself, I had to unfriend someone. This was pre-Facebook, therefore it was actually a proper, real friend and it wasn't as easy as clicking a button. This was a person I knew I would never change because you can't change people unless they want to change themselves. I made the decision to disconnect and limit my dealings with him. We drifted apart and didn't see or talk to one another for probably six or seven years.

I have seen him recently, though, and he has changed – new wife, better job, less stress and so on. Things seem better for him, and perhaps I have better ways of dealing with negativity.

The other main way that negative thoughts and expectations get into your brain is via the media. TV, radio and the Internet will feed you enough ill-will and dubious examples to desensitise you to things that should invoke an emotion.

Take a look at whether you really want to watch or read the news and certain other programs. Be especially careful with what media your children consume, and teach them the difference between reality and what they see on TV.

Looking for hidden agendas

In general we are not taught critical thinking techniques. Unfortunately, this leaves us somewhat at the mercy of advertising, organised religion and politicians.

Advertising

Advertising is great – it tells you about a product and if you actually have a requirement for it then you know where to acquire it. But you have to be careful about hidden messages that seep into your brain, particularly ones that are subconsciously saying 'If you don't drink this soft drink, then you won't be having fun with friends', or 'If you don't use this cleaning product then there will be so many germs in your house that your children might die of something extremely nasty (or you will die of embarrassment)'!

Organised religion

I agonised over whether to include this in the book. As I mentioned earlier, I am certainly not against people believing in a higher power. Almost universally, the message behind all great religions is one of tolerance, empowerment, humility, gratitude and respect. What I am against are people in positions of power in these organisations using religion to feed negative messages, hatred, separateness, distrust and disharmony.

If you belong to a church, temple or spiritual group where the messages are overwhelmingly positive and supportive and empower you to make great decisions and be free of guilt, that is fantastic. Stay there. If not, perhaps you should consider whether religious concepts might be sabotaging the work you are doing with affirmations.

Politicians

It's often been said that the wrong people tend to get in power. Our systems appear to be set up in such a way that being devious is an easy way to rise to the top. Consequently, don't believe everything you hear. There are a lot of people who have a vested interest in keeping you despondent.

Adding visual cues

I already touched on the concept of writing affirmations down. You can leave yourself a note on the bathroom mirror, in the car, in your wallet, on the fridge, on your computer desktop or even tattoo it on your arm. (Have a bit of a think about that last idea before you commit, though, as it's difficult to hit Ctrl-Z for a tattoo.)

Keep on studying

If you want to take this further, NLP (neuro-linguistic programming) can provide additional insights into how your mind works. It can be very effective in conjunction with affirmations for difficult issues such as drug addiction, chronic pain and compulsive disorders. NLP has the concept of a well-formed outcome, which is another way of making sure your affirmations tie in perfectly with what you actually want, not what you think you want.

Bonus: Making your own subliminals tape

I don't know whether this works, but I did it back in the 1990s nevertheless. I don't have any particular anecdotes as to the results of it because I didn't do a control experiment with no subliminals, but I'll tell you what I did and you can do your own research and decide for yourself.

The idea of subliminals is that you have a spoken track underneath another consistent audio track, such as music or a sound effects track like crashing waves. You can't consciously hear the spoken track, but the theory is that your brain picks it up subconsciously.

I was fortunate enough to train as an audio engineer and set up my own recording studio. I had 16-track digital recording with Pro Tools. Back in the mid-'90s it was expensive to do this. Now, it's very cheap with programs like Garageband for Apple Mac.

I got a piece of stereo relaxation music that lasted 30 minutes and digitised it into the computer onto tracks one and two (left and right). You could purchase something like Holosync or any other fairly consistent, relaxing soundtrack – there are a great many options. Try not to purchase something that you will despise later, because you will listen to it quite a lot.

Then I recorded myself saying a few phrases on track three and chopped them into separate sentences to get rid of breathing noises and any other non-essential background noise. I then compressed and normalised the audio.

Compression reduces the difference between the loud and soft parts and is the reason why ads sound louder than TV shows (even though they're technically not). It makes the track more consistently loud. Your compressor will likely be a software compressor in your computer rather than a separate piece of hardware. Use a moderate ratio, e.g. 3:1 to 5:1 with fairly fast attack, and a soft knee. Try to aim for 6-8dB of reduction by adjusting the point at which the compressor starts working (the threshold). This means that when the audio track is playing you will see the meters show up to 6-8dB as it plays. This means you should also add 6-8dB of gain (or make-up gain) to compensate. Don't make it sound unnatural, though.

Normalisation looks for the loudest part of the track. Let's say that it's 80% of its maximum. It will then boost the whole track by the 20% difference.

I assembled the audio snippets on track three in the order I wanted them and then mixed this track (that is, reduced the volume) so it was barely audible under the music. By barely audible, I mean that I could hear the occasional murmur, fricative or sibilant, but I couldn't understand what was being said.

Usually you would just have this running as a single track underneath. However, I thought I might try using the remaining thirteen tracks to have a constant 'wash' of subliminal messaging in the background by starting an affirmation every 0.2 seconds or so.

To do this I simply duplicated track three (the first voice track) onto track four and moved it 0.2 seconds later, and again for tracks 5 to 16. I randomly panned each track (shifted it to some position between the left and right speaker, not dead centre). Once you start adding all those tracks together you'll see why I originally chopped the sentences up and got rid of breathing and other ambient noise – having 13 tracks with breathing and background noise is not desirable!

Looking back at the calculation, if each affirmation was 5 seconds, there are 12 per minute per track. At 30 minutes that's 360 per track. Multiply that by 13 tracks and that's 4680 messages every half an hour!

As I said, I don't know whether it made any difference, but it was cool doing it.

Bear in mind that if you heavily compress your subliminal track as an MP3, the compression will remove a lot of the affirmations data. This is why MP3 files are smaller than raw audio files – because it doesn't encode audio data it thinks you can't hear. You need to keep your tracks at full quality, preferably burned to a CD. Formats like AIFF will retain all the data.

The transition to pure confidence

Affirmations always come about because you have uncertainty. You don't know whether something is going to work out, whether things will be OK, or whether you can do something. The Gap is staring you in the face and you have to somehow get where you want to be.

The pinnacle of affirmations is where it morphs into pure confidence. Occasionally I get this feeling when I think of something I want to achieve, and I think about whether an affirmation might help. Then my mind tells me, 'No, you don't need to affirm that. It's a given that it'll happen.'

I really wish it was that easy with every single affirmation, but it's not. There's still a huge amount of things I haven't achieved, things that don't 'work out', and things that do work out that I think, in hindsight, might have been better if they had been thought through for longer. However, I get this occasional glimpse into how it could be if everything ran with perfect synchronicity; it is pure confidence in a positive outcome.

For those of you who have struggled with your confidence (I am one of them), affirmations will start to make things happen. The more positive things that happen, the greater your confidence will be. Eventually the old you, with its doubts and fears, will be overpowered by the new, confident you.

Affirmations don't define you and affirmations aren't results. Affirmations help you create results by changing your perception of you. You then make everything happen. Affirmations provide the impetus for creating positive change in your life and I truly hope that you can take the time to create that change.

Some bedtime reading

Émile Coué was the father of autosuggestion, which is similar to affirmation.

Louise Hay is an excellent writer and proponent of affirmations.

John Kehoe is arguably one of the pioneers with his *Mind Power* book.

For some serious delving into how we create our lives, try the Seth books by Jane Roberts, particularly *The Nature of Personal Reality* and *Seth Speaks*.

But wait, there's one more thing...

A last important word

Thank you.

Before you go and start creating a more awesome life for yourself, I'd like to say thanks for purchasing this book. I know you could have picked from dozens of self-help books, but you chose this.

And a big thanks for reading through to the end, too. If you liked what you read then I need your help!

Please take a moment to leave a review for this book on Amazon.

If you believe this book is worth sharing, would you take a few seconds to let your friends know about it?

If it helps them with their dreams they'll be grateful to you, as will I.

Once you've started affirming and you see how it positively changes your life, you won't want to stop. I wasn't born with a special set of abilities; I'm not particularly sporty; I don't have the brain of a professor; I've got quite a few personality traits I'm still working on; I've faced some serious adversity with injuries, financial loss and more. The thing is, though, that I know I have absolutely everything I need to improve myself and my situation in life.

When I reached a difficult point writing this book I always returned to the same affirmation: *I am creating massive value*. I hope that this has delivered massive value for you and that you can now go and create massive value for yourself.

If you would like me to notify you when other books become available, send an email to 300affirmations@gmail.com.

Darren

Made in the USA
Columbia, SC
26 October 2017